LEONARD J. ARRINGTON
MORMON HISTORY LECTURE SERIES
No. 21

NARRATING JANE
Telling the Story of an
Early African American Mormon Woman

by Quincy D. Newell

September 24, 2015

Sponsored by

Special Collections & Archives
Merrill-Cazier Library
Utah State University
Logan, Utah

ISBN 978-1-60732-561-1 (paper)
ISBN 978-1-60732-562-8 (ebook)

Published by Merrill-Cazier Library
Distributed by Utah State University Press
Logan, UT 84322

Foreword

F. Ross Peterson

The establishment of a lecture series honoring a library's special collections and a donor to that collection is unique. Utah State University's Merrill-Cazier Library houses the personal and historical collection of Leonard J. Arrington, a renowned scholar of the American West. As part of Arrington's gift to the university, he requested that the university's historical collection become the focus for an annual lecture on an aspect of Mormon history. Utah State agreed to the request and in 1995 inaugurated the annual Leonard J. Arrington Mormon History Lecture.

Utah State University's Special Collections and Archives is ideally suited as the host for the lecture series. The state's land grant university began collecting records very early, and in the 1960s became a major depository for Utah and Mormon records. Leonard and his wife Grace joined the USU faculty and family in 1946, and the Arringtons and their colleagues worked to collect original diaries, journals, letters, and photographs.

Although trained as an economist at the University of North Carolina, Arrington became a Mormon historian of international repute. Working with numerous colleagues, the Twin Falls, Idaho, native produced the classic *Great Basin Kingdom: An Economic History of the Latter-day Saints* in 1958. Utilizing available collections at USU, Arrington embarked on a prolific publishing and editing career. He and his close ally, Dr. S. George Ellsworth, helped organize the Western History Association, and they created the *Western Historical Quarterly* as the scholarly voice of the WHA. While serving with Ellsworth as editor of the new journal, Arrington also helped both the Mormon History Association and the independent journal *Dialogue*.

One of Arrington's great talents was to encourage and inspire other scholars or writers. While he worked on biographies or institutional histories, he employed many young scholars as researchers. He fostered many careers as well as arranged for the publication of numerous books and articles.

In 1973, Arrington accepted appointments as the official historian of the Church of Jesus Christ of Latter-day Saints and the Lemuel Redd Chair of Western History at Brigham Young University. More and more Arrington focused on Mormon, rather than economic, historical topics. His own career flourished with the publication of *The Mormon Experience*, co-authored with Davis Bitton, and *American Moses: A Biography of Brigham Young*. He and his staff produced many research papers and position papers for the LDS Church as well. Nevertheless, tension developed over the historical process, and Arrington chose to move full time to BYU with his entire staff. The Joseph Fielding Smith Institute of History was established, and Leonard continued to mentor new scholars as well as publish biographies. He also produced a very significant two-volume study, *The History of Idaho*.

After Grace Arrington passed away, Leonard married Harriet Horne of Salt Lake City. They made the decision to deposit the vast Arrington collection of research documents, letters, files, books, and journals at Utah State University. The Leonard J. Arrington Historical Archives is part of the university's Special Collections. The Arrington Lecture Committee works with Special Collections to sponsor the annual lecture.

About the Author

Quincy D. Newell is an associate professor of religious studies at Hamilton College in Clinton, New York, where she studies and teaches about American religions. Her research focuses on the religious history of the American West, and she has published extensively in this area. She earned her bachelor's degree from Amherst College, and her M.A. and Ph.D. from the University of North Carolina at Chapel Hill. A native Oregonian, she headed back to the West in 2004 to teach at the University of Wyoming, where she was on the faculty for eleven years. Newell is the author of *Constructing Lives at Mission San Francisco: Native Californians and Hispanic Colonists, 1776-1821* (University of New Mexico Press, 2009) and the co-editor of *New Perspectives in Mormon Studies: Creating and Crossing Boundaries* (University of Oklahoma Press, 2013). Her current projects concern the religious experiences of nineteenth-century African American and Native American Mormons.

NARRATING JANE

Introduction

It is an honor to have been selected to give the 21ˢᵗ annual Arrington lecture. This annual lecture honors Leonard Arrington, a giant in the field of Mormon history. Arrington and I share an alma mater—he took his Ph.D. in economics at the University of North Carolina at Chapel Hill in 1952. His first book, *Great Basin Kingdom: An Economic History of the Latter-day Saints, 1830-1900,* was based on his dissertation.[1] The year Professor Arrington died, I began my graduate work at the University of North Carolina at Chapel Hill. When I got to my qualifying exams, *Great Basin Kingdom* was one of the "classics" on my reading list. It stuck with me, both for all that it offered and for that which was missing, and, in a way, you might say that Arrington's book is what enticed me into the field of Mormon Studies.

You see, *Great Basin Kingdom* deals with production and consumption, trade and taxes, labor and management. One thing it does not address is slavery—which left me flummoxed when I learned that some nineteenth-century Mormons held slaves and that they brought those slaves with them when they gathered to Zion. At that point, I had not yet learned just how complicated was the legal status of those African American men and women.[2] All I knew was that slavery is a topic that would generally be treated under the heading of economic history, and it was not in *Great Basin Kingdom.* The index was no help—there were no black people in the book. I was intrigued.

But, as is the case for many graduate students and junior professors, other matters pressed more urgently, so I filed the question of race in early Mormonism away for later. When I finally had the opportunity to return to it, I set to work shaping a book around the question of what it was like to be a Mormon of color in the nineteenth century, focusing on African American and Native American Mormons. One woman, in particular, kept showing up in my research—a woman named Jane Elizabeth Manning James.[3]

Jane was born in Connecticut around 1822.[4] Her mother had been enslaved, but Jane was free from her birth. As a young girl, she went to work for a wealthy white family in a nearby town. She joined the local Congregational church when she was about twenty—but within about a year, she heard a Mormon missionary preach and was won over. She accepted LDS baptism and persuaded her family to do so as well. In 1843, the Mannings and several other converts—both black and white—set out for Nauvoo. They travelled by boat, but the black passengers were refused passage beyond Buffalo. They walked the rest of the way, about nine hundred miles, to Nauvoo. They went to the Smiths' Mansion House, where, Jane later claimed, she recognized Joseph Smith because she had seen him in a vision.[5]

Once there, Jane took a job working for Joseph and Emma Smith as a domestic servant—the same work she had done in Connecticut. The first time she washed Joseph's temple robes, Jane went into a trance. She said later that while she was in that ecstatic state, the Holy Spirit gave her to know that these robes had to do with "the new name that is given the Saints that the world knows not of."[6] Throughout her life, Jane said she also experienced supernatural healings—both as the recipient of healing and as an agent of it—and she spoke in tongues. In Mormonism, Jane had found a place where her ecstatic experiences were validated and, at least most of the time, encouraged.[7]

Jane brought her young son, Sylvester, with her from Connecticut. We do not know who Sylvester's biological father was, though Jane's brother was reported to have claimed that the man was a white preacher.[8] In Nauvoo, Jane married Isaac James, a black Mormon convert from New Jersey, and, with Isaac and Sylvester, she set out for Utah in one of the first companies to reach the Salt Lake Valley. Jane and Isaac had several more children and did fairly well for themselves in Salt Lake. At various times, they both appear to have worked for Brigham Young; they bought land in the city and acquired farm animals and implements. But in 1870, Isaac and Jane divorced.[9] Isaac left the city, apparently with a white fortune teller.[10] Jane remained behind. Some evidence indicates that Jane remarried in about 1874: Jane began signing her name and appearing in public records as "Jane Elizabeth Manning Perkins," adopting the surname of her apparent husband, another black Mormon named Frank Perkins. However, the relationship did not last, and by 1877, Jane had returned to using "James" as her surname.[11] She was baptized for her dead, and she started to request temple privileges.[12] She wanted her endowments, and she wanted to be sealed in marriage. At various points, she requested marriage sealing to Walker Lewis, a black priesthood holder, and to Isaac James. Most of all, she wanted to be sealed as a child to Joseph Smith.[13] This last request was not unusual: lots of Latter-day Saints at the time were asking for, and receiving, the same thing.[14] Jane said that Emma Smith had offered this opportunity to her in Nauvoo and that she had turned it down at the time because she did not understand. But she wanted to change her mind now: please, could she be sealed to Joseph as a child?

Over and over, Jane made this request. She visited church leaders in their homes; she wrote letters; she asked influential women to write on her behalf.

In the midst of Jane's campaign to receive her endowments and be sealed, Isaac returned. He had been away for two decades, and he died less than a year after coming back to Salt Lake City. Jane held his funeral at her house. And still, she petitioned to be sealed to Joseph Smith as a child.

Church leaders kept saying no: they were clearly uncomfortable sealing a black person to a white one in a parent-child relationship, creating an interracial family.[15] But finally, they found a compromise: they offered Jane the opportunity to be sealed to Joseph Smith as a servant. She apparently agreed, because a ceremony was created and performed—with Zina Young acting as proxy for Jane, even though Jane was alive and well.[16] Still, sealing as a servant was not enough. Quorum of the Twelve minutes tell us that she returned to petitioning for an adoption sealing after that—her campaign lasted pretty much until her death in 1908.[17]

With a life story like that, you can see why I am fascinated by Jane. But I am also deeply interested in the ways Latter-day Saints talk about Jane, the ways they tell her story to each other, and that is where I will focus in the rest of this essay.

Jane's story was largely forgotten for about half a century after her death. In the 1960s and 1970s a few pieces appeared, laying out her biography and digging up some of the documentary evidence connected to her life.[18] But with one exception, which I will discuss shortly, talk about Jane was infrequent, and publications were not widely circulated. All that changed around the turn of the millennium. Suddenly, U.S. Mormons started talking about Jane incessantly. There were books, articles, novels, plays, blogs, films, monuments, even fine art.[19] Jane became comparatively well known, and Latter-day Saints told her story over and over again. What is curious to me is that Jane's current popularity is far larger than her role in LDS history actually warrants. This is not simply a manifestation of the general LDS enthusiasm for Mormon history—if it were, it would have shown up much earlier. So what explains the timing and the shape of this recent Jane James-mania? Why is she discussed so widely now, when she hardly merited a footnote in the 1960s or 1970s, and why do Latter-day Saints tell her story in the ways that they do?

I will argue that Jane's story performs several functions for modern Latter-day Saints. First, for individual Latter-day Saints, Jane's story provides a model for living a devout life through trying circumstances. Jane's example is especially applicable in the lives of Latter-day Saint women. Her story also helps revitalize the LDS faith by confirming its truth and returning some of the enchantment to it in a thoroughly disenchanted world.[20]

Second, on an institutional level, Jane's story helps the LDS church construct a story of its past that positions the church optimally for the future. Jane's story drives home the point that the LDS church is racially diverse, and makes the case that it always has been a multi-racial church. Moreover, Jane's relationship with Joseph Smith—which she portrayed as particularly close and friendly—helps depict Smith as a non-racist. Thus, talking about Jane allows the church to walk away from its problematic racial past and shift attention to the social norms it carries into the future.

Representing Jane

When Latter-day Saints talk about Jane, they make two important kinds of moves. First, they universalize Jane's story. Even though she gets Mormons' attention because she was an African American convert in a time when African American Mormons were pretty unusual, some of the ways in which Mormons talk about Jane drain her story of that racial particularity, denying the significance of race and focusing, instead, on Jane's identities as a woman and a mother. This universalization of Jane's story makes her an accessible example of good LDS living—she becomes someone that the largely white American Mormon audience for her story can and should emulate and she especially becomes a model of LDS femininity. Secondly, Mormons who talk about Jane dwell in her racial particularity. However, they do so by emphasizing characteristics that are stereotypically associated with African Americans, characteristics that are not necessarily historically correct in Jane's case—so they paint Jane with their *idea* of blackness rather than attending to Jane's actual *experience.* Drawing on longstanding cultural associations that link black people with primitiveness, those who narrate Jane's story in this way use those associations to confirm Mormonism's truth claims, and they use the exoticism of the primitive to make the faith feel a bit less like the rational, civilized, workaday world—a bit more enchanted.[21] I will discuss each of these moves in turn—first the universalizing, and then the particularizing.

Universalizing

As far as I have been able to tell, the first official Church treatment of Jane James's life was a 1979 article in *Ensign* by Linda King Newell and Valeen Tippetts Avery. The article was called "Jane Manning James: Black Saint, 1847 Pioneer."[22] The aspects of Jane's life that the subtitle highlighted might, at first glance, have singled her out as utterly unique. However, Newell and Avery skillfully wove their tale in such a way that their audience—mostly white Mormons—was able to find in Jane a model to emulate.[23]

Newell and Avery's account was important because it was the first really widely available narration of Jane's life, and, because it appeared in *Ensign*, it bore the church's official stamp of approval, so to speak. Not surprisingly then, this article became the model for many of the later renditions of Jane's life.[24]

Newell and Avery presented a Jane James who was particularly fitted for the late-twentieth-century church. They omitted several of the details I mentioned earlier, even though those details were available in the sources they consulted.[25] For example, they did not talk about Jane's ecstatic experiences of visions and dreams, or speaking in tongues. They also did not discuss her relationship with Frank Perkins after her divorce from Isaac James, nor did they bring up the question of her first child's father.[26] They did not talk about Jane's requests to be sealed to Joseph Smith, or the fact that she was sealed to him as a servant.[27]

Every historian must omit some details, and Newell and Avery were likely working with a pretty strict word limit for this *Ensign* article. But these omissions were not just random, space-saving cuts. They fit a pattern that suggests a thoughtful shaping of Jane's image, much as a photographer might strategically crop a photo to present her subject in the clearest way possible. The key to the pattern was in that subtitle: "Black Saint, 1847 Pioneer."[28] I will focus first on the "Saint" and "Pioneer" aspects presented here, and then return to the question of Jane's blackness.

When she told her own life story, Jane presented herself as something of a religious virtuoso. She spoke in tongues early—as soon as she converted to Mormonism—and often, in meetings of the Retrenchment Society in the late nineteenth century.[29] She healed herself and others by faith, without the aid of the priesthood.[30] She received sacred knowledge from the Holy Spirit about temple ceremonies from which church leaders excluded her.[31] These ecstatic religious experiences were important to Jane and to her sense of who she was as a Latter-day Saint. They were not, however, all that unusual in her day. Other people did the same things—they spoke in tongues, they healed and received healing through supernatural means, they had visions and received divine communications.[32]

Today, Latter-day Saints understand the gift of tongues to refer primarily to "the ability of missionaries to learn foreign languages quickly."[33] Jane James and her contemporaries understood it completely differently. To them, Orson Pratt wrote, speaking in tongues was an assurance "not only of the truth of the doctrine [of the church], but that they themselves were accepted of God."[34] Nineteenth-century Latter-day Saints understood the gift of tongues to come in two forms: *glossolalia*, or speaking in an unknown language, often identified as the language of Adam; and *xenoglossia*, or speaking in human languages of which the speaker otherwise has no knowledge. Xenoglossia was of great value in the Latter-day Saints' missionary work, but glossolalia was regularly manifested in LDS congregations, and it is this form of tongues that Jane experienced.

Today, you would be hard pressed to find a Latter-day Saint who has experienced glossolalia—unless she or he was a convert from Pentecostalism. Healings are still sought, but in acute cases, like one that Jane talked about involving open wounds,[35] Latter-day Saints are likely to get medical help rather than relying solely on prayer. And Latter-day Saints certainly seek, and expect to receive, divine communications—but reports of trances and visions are infrequent. Jane's version of Mormonism—one that looked practically Pentecostal in its spiritual manifestations—has faded away, replaced by a buttoned-down, correlated, respectable form of the faith.[36] Those ecstatic experiences are now associated, in American culture, with the religions of the disinherited, America's economically marginalized, and often racially stigmatized, groups—think snake handlers, Voudou priestesses, and Holy Rollers.

In their profile, Newell and Avery distanced Jane from those marginal populations and fit her into the mold of this later, respectable form of Mormonism by omitting virtually all of her ecstatic religious experiences. Gone were the instances of speaking in tongues; gone, the trance over Joseph Smith's temple robes; even most of the healings disappeared from the narrative. What remained was a Jane James who might easily worship with the readers of Newell and Avery's article, a woman readers could almost imagine sitting next to them in Sunday School or Relief Society.

Strategic omissions, like those that de-emphasized Jane's image as a religious virtuoso, also enabled Newell and Avery to emphasize her moral virtues. By omitting the details of Jane's sexual life that did not fit late-twentieth-century LDS behavioral standards—the fact that her first child was born out of wedlock, and the fact that she had a relationship with another man after her divorce, in particular—Newell and Avery sanitized Jane's history and strengthened the image of Jane as an exemplary Mormon woman. Newell and Avery repeatedly emphasized Jane's Mormon values and pioneer virtues: she "endured the hardships of pioneer life," and she had a "sense of adventure" and "courage."[37] She had great "faith" that helped her keep going through the hardships of her journey to Nauvoo, and, once the Saints reached Utah, Jane and her family demonstrated "hard work, thrift, and perseverance" that "helped them acquire a home and farm animals."[38] At the end of her life, as Newell and Avery related it, Jane continued to be "steadfast," with "undaunted faith" and "loving generosity."[39]

Newell and Avery characterized Jane's repeated petitions for sealings as growing out of these two characteristics—faith and generosity. In their telling, she "respectfully requested permission from the First Presidency for her family to be sealed to her."[40] This gloss on the story omitted Jane's requests to be sealed to the black priesthood holder Walker Lewis—which might have been seen as unfaithful to her ex-husband Isaac (despite their divorce), as well as her requests to be sealed to Joseph Smith as a child and her requests to receive her endowment, which might have raised uncomfortable questions about the racial policies of the nineteenth-century church.[41] Newell and Avery also omitted entirely Jane's sealing to Joseph Smith as a servant. The conclusion of their discussion of Jane's requests showed the reader that Jane's faithful obedience was ultimately rewarded: "Although . . . permission [for sealings] was denied at the time," they wrote, "Jane was able to be baptized for her kindred dead. (Temple work—endowments and sealings—has recently been done for Jane and her family.)"[42]

Importantly, Jane's model of faithful living, as seen in Newell and Avery's profile, was available to Latter-day Saints regardless of their racial identities. Even though the subtitle of the article made a point of noting that Jane was a "*Black* Saint" (my emphasis), Newell and Avery's discussion of that identity was thin. To be sure, Newell and Avery highlighted Jane's race at key moments throughout the profile. In the first paragraph, which described Jane's arrival in Nauvoo with her traveling companions, Jane was "a free black woman."[43] Describing Joseph Smith's campaign for president in 1844, Newell and Avery speculated that "Jane, in particular, must have felt a sense of personal importance that one of the planks of the platform was a strong proclamation to 'Break off the shackles from the . . . black man, and hire him to labor like other human beings.'"[44] Newell and Avery identified Jane's suitors as black, and they described Jane and her family on the trek to Utah in heroic, racialized terms: "Black faces turned resolutely toward the west; Jane and Isaac James, their son Silas, and Jane's son Sylvester, were counted in the lead company of the main encampment."[45] Newell and Avery summed up Jane's life at the end of their profile by stating that "Throughout her life, Jane maintained her identification as both a black and a Mormon."[46] Still, blackness was a cosmetic difference here. Newell and Avery did not explore the ways in which blackness shaped Jane's experience as a Latter-day Saint—how being a "Black Saint" might have been different than being a white one.[47] The implication was that racial identity was not religiously meaningful—not in Newell and Avery's time, nor in Jane James's time.

I have claimed that Newell and Avery portrayed Jane as a model for Latter-day Saints in general, but this version of Jane worked particularly well as a model of Latter-day Saint femininity. Newell and Avery's article came out as the United States debated the Equal Rights Amendment, sometimes in very heated terms. In contrast to the model of outspoken, activist femininity offered at the time by women like Sonia Johnson, Newell and Avery's portrait of Jane as a virtuous, obedient, and steadfastly faithful woman offered an alternative version of pioneering Mormon womanhood.[48] Newell and Avery closed with a quotation from Jane's autobiography: "I want to say right here, that my faith in the gospel of Jesus Christ, as taught by the Church of Jesus Christ of Latter-day Saints, is as strong today, nay, it is if possible stronger than it was the day I was first baptized. I pay my tithes and offerings, keep the word of wisdom, I go to bed early and rise early, I try in my feeble way to set a good example to all."[49] The implication, of course, was that this "Black Saint" and "1847 Pioneer" *did* set a good example for everyone, in her powerful faith, her

Figure 1. When the monument to Jane James was first created in 1999, it bore only this image of Jane sharing flour with Eliza Lyman. Photo by Quincy D. Newell.

patient obedience to priesthood authority, and her modest life of hard work, thrift, and loving generosity.

I have lingered on Newell and Avery's article because it was so important in shaping the way Jane James has been portrayed in the LDS Church since the article's publication. They set a pattern—of noting Jane's race but making it cosmetic at most and of focusing more on the ways Jane lived up to LDS ideals of femininity than on how race shaped her experience as a Latter-day Saint. That pattern is readily apparent in twenty-first century treatments of Jane's life story as well.

A monument placed at Jane James's grave may be the most tangible example of the way in which Jane's life has been drained of its racial particularity in favor of emphasis on more "universal" aspects of her story. The monument is a relatively modest block of granite with brass plaques on both sides. When it was first placed at Jane's grave in the Salt Lake City Cemetery in 1999, the monument included only one of these plaques, a bronze relief depicting Jane sharing half of her flour with Eliza Partridge Lyman, a white woman (figure 1).[50] In 2005, the monument was completed with the addition of the second plaque on the opposite side of the granite block (figure 2).

This plaque was all text, interspersing quotations from Jane's autobiography with selected facts about her life:

JANE ELIZABETH MANNING JAMES

"I try in my feeble way to set a good example for all."
Born free in 1882, Fairfield County, Connecticut
Baptized LDS in 1841, she led a group of family members to
Nauvoo, Illinois in 1843
"Our feet cracked open and bled until you could see the whole prints
of our feet with blood on the ground"
Jane lived with Joseph, Emma and Mother Smith
"Brother Joseph sat down by me and said, 'God bless you,
you are among friends."
Married Isaac James around 1845
Arrived in Salt Lake September 22, 1847
"Oh how I suffered of cold and hunger, but the Lord gave us faith
and grace to stand it all."
Shared half her flour with Eliza Partridge Lyman,
who was near starving.
Died April 16, 1908, outliving all but two of her eight children
"But we went on our way rejoicing, singing hymns, and thanking God
for His infinite goodness and mercy to us."[51]

The only textual reference to Jane's racial identity was the statement that she was "born free," implying that the opposite was possible—and thus, suggesting Jane's race through the potential for her enslavement. Careful observers might infer Jane's race from her stereotypically African American facial structure in the image on the opposite side, though nothing specified which figure represented Jane. Thus, although Jane was memorialized in this monument specifically because she was an African American Latter-day Saint, her race remained unspoken and other attributes again took center stage.

The monument presented a Jane James whose behavior fit the mold for twentieth- and twenty-first-century Latter-day Sainthood. Like Newell and Avery's profile, this representation of Jane removed her ecstatic religious experiences from view, focusing instead on her exemplary moral qualities. The opening and closing quotations controlled the interpretation of the text, informing the reader that Jane was to be taken as a "good example" and that her life was to be seen as an instantiation of God's "infinite

Figure 2. In 2005, a second plaque was affixed to the monument to Jane James in the Salt Lake City Cemetery. Photo by Quincy D. Newell.

goodness and mercy." The overwhelming theme of this abbreviated version of Jane's life was family: the text moved Jane from one family grouping to another, beginning with her biological family, continuing with Joseph Smith's family, and ending with Jane's husband and children. The deaths of most of her children by the end of her life set up the final lesson for the reader: in the face of overwhelming loss, exemplary Latter-day Saints go "on [their] way rejoicing, singing hymns, and thanking God for his infinite goodness and mercy to [them]."

The 2005 rededication service for the monument reinforced this emphasis on family: the monument was dedicated not only to Jane, but also to her family. At the same time, a headstone was placed at Jane's grave engraved with the words "IN MEMORY OF Jane and Isaac James and Family" on one side (figure 3) and, on the other side, "Sacred to the memory of the children of Jane and Isaac James," with the names of eight children, and "Isaac and Jane's grandchildren buried here" with the names of four grandchildren (figure 4).

Figure 3. A headstone placed at Jane's grave in 2005 expanded the monument to include her husband and children. Photo by Quincy D. Newell.

Elder Alexander B. Morrison, an *emeritus* member of the First Quorum of the Seventy, gave the dedicatory prayer at the service. Morrison's prayer emphasized the concept of family: the final petition asked that the monument be a place where people could "contemplate the eternal nature of the family, and of sacred bonds which bind parents and children together through all generations of time."[52] Here again, Jane's race mattered little: instead, her role as mother and grandmother was the most salient feature of her identity, placing her in relation to her children and grandchildren.

That last petition in Morrison's prayer practically demands that we read his words, and the monument and ceremony more generally, in light of the First Presidency's 1995 statement "The Family: A Proclamation to the World," which articulated a very specific understanding of the composition and function of families, and the roles of family members.[53] Both the plaque placed in 2005 and the rededication ceremony that year portrayed Jane as someone who lived up to the principles of the proclamation: she married Isaac James and—as far as the reader of the plaque can tell—bore and raised eight children with him. And, since there was no mention of

Figure 4. The headstone placed in 2005 included not only Jane and Isaac James, but also Jane's children and grandchildren. Photo by Quincy D. Newell.

Isaac and Jane's divorce or Jane's subsequent relationship with Frank Perkins, readers were left to assume that Jane and Isaac fulfilled the proclamation's mandate of "honor[ing] marital vows with complete fidelity."[54] Here, as in Newell and Avery's article earlier, Jane's practice of Mormonism was recognizable to twenty-first-century Latter-day Saints, and her racial identity was treated as irrelevant. The elimination of unfamiliar religious practices like speaking in tongues and of specific racial experiences like Jane's exclusion from most temple ceremonies, and the sanitizing of Jane's sexual history rendered her an accessible moral example for twenty-first century Latter-day Saints—and especially for women.

Particularizing

The other move that Latter-day Saints make when they tell Jane's story is to dwell on her racial particularity. This move is complicated because the ways narrators imagine and signal Jane's blackness often have very little to do with Jane's actual experience. Instead, those who tell Jane's story in this way draw on longstanding stereotypes of blackness, marking

Jane's race by giving her characteristics stereotypically associated with black people.

One of most pervasive stereotypes characterizes people of African descent as "primitive." The idea of "the primitive" has a long history in European and American discourse and it carries a host of connotations. As applied to "religion," for example, the term "primitive" has long denoted beliefs and practices that seem unscientific, irrational, sometimes downright magical.[55] Jane's ecstatic religious experiences fit right into this category, which helps explain why they were glossed over in narratives that sought to universalize her experience and make her a respectable model for twenty-first-century Mormons.

The image of black people as primitive also slides easily into conceptions of African Americans as childlike: uneducated, simple, untroubled by the worries of modern civilization.[56] For example, in July 2005, the Pioneer Chapter of the National Society of the Sons of Utah Pioneers honored Jane James as an "Exemplar of Virtue and Faith." The citation, a part of the annual "Days of '47 Sunrise Service" held in the Assembly Hall on Temple Square in Salt Lake City, took up the entire reverse side of the program for its rehearsal of Jane's life story and its extraction of morals from that narrative.[57] The narrative began with Jane seeing Joseph Smith in a dream and recognizing him as a prophet. On that basis, she requested baptism. Next, according to the text, "She was handed the Book of Mormon but couldn't read it. But the book felt good in her hands. She understood its message." In point of fact, we are uncertain about Jane's literacy. She claimed to be able to both read and write, though all of her letters that survive were actually written by other people, and the evidence for her ability to read is sketchy, at best. It would not have been unreasonable, then, to suggest that Jane could not read the Book of Mormon, but this passage did much more than that. The tactile detail of Jane's encounter with the Book of Mormon—"The book felt good in her hands"—substituted for a more intellectual understanding of the message of the scripture.[58] Instead, Jane magically absorbed the message of the book. This version of the story situated Jane as uneducated, magical, and childlike—a primitive.

By portraying Jane in this way, the citation validated Mormonism's truth claims. Casting Jane's acceptance of Mormonism as the result of a dream and her understanding of its message as non-intellectual were both narrative strategies that located Jane's choice to become LDS in a prerational realm. She did not overthink this decision. In fact, in this version, she did not really *think* about it at all. Uncorrupted by modern, secular culture, Jane instinctively recognized Joseph Smith as a prophet, and Mormonism as the true faith. Modern readers, the text suggested, doubted the message of Mormonism only because their overly intellectual approach obscured the simple truth.

Even as the Sons of Utah Pioneers citation portrayed Jane as a childlike figure, it also transformed her into a surrogate mother, welcoming readers into her maternal embrace. Here the text invoked another ubiquitous stereotype of African American women: the Mammy figure. Rooted in southern slavery, the character of the black Mammy is perhaps most familiar to Americans in her guise as Aunt Jemima—but the Mammy is much more than a short-order cook. The Mammy figure represents black women as selfless, sexless, and nurturing to those around them—usually and most especially to the children of the white families for whom they work.[59] The Sons of Utah Pioneers citation set Jane up for this role in its narration of her charity to Eliza Lyman: "Though Jane herself was poverty stricken and faced the pain of hearing her own children crying from hunger which she could not assuage," the citation reads, "yet she had the love and found the courage to share half of her flour with a white pioneer who had less than she." Jane also extended that maternal love to her ex-husband when he returned from twenty years away. The citation asserts that "[Jane] welcomed [Isaac] back when he returned and he died enfolded in her love." Now, the citation claimed, Jane's motherly love was available to modern Latter-day Saints: "Now new generations are coming to know this virtuous woman. Many of us have become Jane's and Emma's and Joseph's children by spiritual yearning."[60] As she did with her husband, Jane would enfold believers—black or white—in her love. As she did with Eliza Lyman, she would give generously of herself, so that modern Mormons would have what they needed as well.[61]

Connecting with Jane in both her "primitive child" and her "spiritual Mammy" forms might be a very attractive possibility for contemporary Latter-day Saints whose busy, workaday lives lack what some scholars refer to as the "enchantment" of the premodern world.[62] In this "disenchanted," modern world, the divine is relegated to a back seat. We explain the causes of disease and health by referring to germs and antibodies, not sin and repentance; we explicate natural disasters by discussing climate change or tectonic plates rather than divine judgment; we describe political events in terms of economic systems and social movements rather than prophecy and divine justice. In other words, society at large no longer acknowledges the divine as the moving force behind our world. Faith is individual, private, and optional, instead of communal, public, and taken for granted. The magic is gone.

Connecting to Jane re-enchants that world just a little bit. Jane's primitive, childlike belief and her ecstatic experiences offer a kind of exotic overlay to Mormonism. She seems a little closer to the divine, a little more able to slip into that magical world where miracles happen on a regular basis. Through Jane, modern Mormons get a little closer to that world themselves. And, as a spiritual mammy, Jane welcomes her modern Mormon children with open arms, enfolding them in her love and giving them a refuge from their disenchanted, modern world.

Representing Joseph

I have argued that Jane's story offers individual Latter-day Saints—and especially women—a model for living a life of faith and a chance to imbue that faith with a sense of enchantment and conviction. But because Jane James was an early African American convert to Mormonism, her story also presents Latter-day Saints with an opportunity to think about race in the context of the church's history.

In the late twentieth and early twenty-first centuries, the LDS Church has struggled with its legacy on race, fighting to change outsiders' perceptions that the church was and is a racist institution that continues to discriminate against people of African descent. Including Jane in authorized retellings of LDS history is a natural way for the church to bolster these efforts by presenting the church as racially diverse, and welcoming to black people, since its earliest days. Every summer, Mormons put on pageants around the U.S. (and around the globe) depicting their history. In 2005, the Nauvoo pageant got a makeover—a whole new script, written under the supervision of LDS Church leadership.[63] The new version not only included Jane James but gave her a speaking role. Similarly, the official church film about the prophet, *Joseph Smith: Prophet of the Restoration*, also released in 2005, represented Smith himself bandaging the bloody feet of one of Jane's black traveling companions after they arrived in Nauvoo, as he spoke with Jane. Jane's role in both of these historical dramas visually asserted the racial diversity of the church.[64]

But one of the most striking features of Latter-day Saint talk about Jane James is the way in which it provides opportunities for Latter-day Saints to talk about Joseph Smith—and this, I think, is the key to understanding the timing of this explosion of interest in Jane. It is no coincidence that most of the examples I have discussed in this essay came from 2005, the bicentennial of Joseph Smith's birth and thus a key moment to reflect on the life of the prophet and his lessons for the modern church. Talking about Joseph by talking about Jane gives Latter-day Saints the opportunity to remember the prophet in ways that position the church for the future.

When it came to race, Joseph Smith was, not surprisingly, a man of his times. It is worth remembering that during Joseph Smith's lifetime, there was no broad consensus about the "Christian" position on race or race-based slavery, as there is now. Rather, there was an ongoing debate on those questions, with extremists on both sides and, probably, most folks somewhere in the middle.[65] Smith was fairly consistent in his opposition to slavery, but he found the demands of the abolitionists too extreme, proposing instead that enslaved people be purchased and freed. Smith seemed to recognize the innate equality of black and white people, but in almost the same breath, he suggested African Americans should be "confine[d]. . . by strict Laws to their own Species," a statement historian Richard Bushman interpreted as an expression of opposition to interracial marriage.[66] Relatively progressive for the early nineteenth century, Smith's racial attitudes are a little harder to digest in the twenty-first century. The story of Jane James offers a remedy. For example, Jane's interactions with Joseph Smith in the church film *Joseph Smith: The Prophet of the Restoration* implicitly indicated that Joseph did not see race as a barrier to religious or social bonds.[67]

Like that film, explicit talk about Joseph Smith in the context of Jane's story usually presents him as friendly and welcoming to her and her family, following Jane's own depiction of the prophet. Jane had good reasons for representing Joseph in this way: by emphasizing her intimacy with the prophet and his family and the ways in which Joseph made her welcome, Jane hoped to persuade church leaders to grant her the endowments and sealings she so deeply desired.[68] Twenty-first-century commentators have different concerns: their depictions of the prophet suggest that they hope to rehabilitate the prophet's image, eliminating the ambivalences in his statements on race and rendering him a prophet fit for the twenty-first century—friendly, welcoming, and racially tolerant. One standard strategy is to suggest that Joseph understood what it was like to be black in nineteenth-century America, because he, too, had suffered persecution. For example, the citation proclaiming Jane an "Exemplar of Virtue and Faith" at the Sons of Utah Pioneers' 2005 Pioneer Day Sunrise Service stated, "There was a powerful bond among Joseph, Emma, and Jane. All three knew persecution. All three knew they were of the same blood, the blood of Israel."[69] Equating the suffering of Joseph Smith, Emma Smith, and Jane James, this narrative argued that their shared knowledge of persecution brought the three together and gave them a common kinship.

In her remarks at the 2005 rededication of Jane's monument, Brigham Young University Professor Susan Easton Black also drew a parallel between the prejudice and discrimination that nineteenth-century African Americans faced, and what Joseph Smith experienced. "The Prophet," she stated, "knew much of prejudicial treatment. He had endured tarring and feathering, an extermination order, and imprisonment in Independence, Richmond, and Liberty Jail. Yet he knew that there was a God in heaven and that God in heaven had sent to him a choice daughter in the 1840s named Jane Manning." In this version, Joseph Smith experienced prejudice like the black people of his day (tarring and feathering, extermination orders, and unjust imprisonment) and he bucked social norms by embracing Jane James as his heaven-sent daughter. Susan Easton Black concluded, "The continuum of [Jane's] life, much [like] the life of Joseph Smith, focused on her faith."[70] In other words, Jane and Joseph were a lot alike—even though Jane was black and Joseph was white, both experienced prejudice and both "focused on . . . faith."

Black's logic here follows the same path as theologian James Cone's when he declared that "Christ is black"[71] and author Toni Morrison's when she described Bill Clinton as the United States' "first black president."[72] For Cone, the defining characteristic of blackness in twentieth-century America was oppression: "In America," he wrote, "blacks are oppressed because of their blackness." But, he continued, "the Church knows that what is shame to the world is holiness to God. Black is holy, that is, it is a symbol of God's presence in history on behalf of the oppressed man." Cone concluded, "Therefore Christ is black because he is oppressed, and oppressed because he is black."[73] Similarly, Toni Morrison wrote in *The New Yorker* in fall of 1998 that Bill Clinton was "our first black President" for two reasons. First, he "display[ed] almost every trope of blackness: single-parent household, born poor, working-class, saxophone-playing, McDonald's-and-junk-food-loving boy from Arkansas." Second, "the President's body, his privacy, his unpoliced sexuality became the focus of . . . persecution, . . . he was metaphorically seized and body-searched."[74] So for Cone, blackness is about siding with the oppressed, and for Morrison, it is about being treated like black people. Now recall Susan Easton Black's description of Joseph Smith: "He had endured tarring and feathering, an extermination order, and imprisonment . . . . Yet he knew that there was a God in heaven and that God . . . had sent to him a choice daughter . . . named Jane Manning." That description, I think, made Joseph Smith the LDS Church's very first "black Mormon." As Susan Easton Black—and other commentators, too—have framed Joseph Smith's story, he was treated like black people, fulfilling Toni Morrison's criterion for blackness, and he sided with Jane James and other black people, fulfilling James Cone's requirements. I do not mean to imply that Susan Easton Black would endorse this conclusion; I simply want to point out the logic of equating the persecution Joseph Smith encountered with the race-based oppression that African Americans faced. What better way to rehabilitate Joseph Smith's racial attitudes than to make him black in all but skin color? In this way, Smith becomes the kind of founder of whom modern Latter-day Saints can be proud: one who loves all human beings, regardless of race, and who calls them to a racially egalitarian future.

Conclusion

Several years ago, Kathleen Flake argued that Joseph F. Smith and the other leaders of the LDS Church used events surrounding the first centennial of Joseph Smith's birth to ease the church's transition into the twentieth century. Emphasizing the church's foundations in "restored church order, divine authority, and continuing revelation,"[75] then-President Smith and his colleagues shifted the church's focus from the founder's last revelation, on celestial marriage, to his first one—the experience now known as the First Vision. This strategy, Flake argued, allowed the church to finesse the suspension of plural marriage without rejecting the doctrine outright; to claim a place in the American nation without sacrificing Mormonism's strong corporate identity.[76]

Paying attention to talk about and representations of Jane James allows us to see a similar shift taking place around the second centennial of the prophet's birth. This time, the church faced somewhat different issues: first, how to leave behind the racism of the priesthood and temple restrictions and thus become more like the more racially progressive society outside the church; and second, how to maintain its relatively conservative stance on gender and family roles as the society around it increasingly rejected those ideals. Part of the solution has been a strategy of redirection. For all the jubilation that attended its reception and canonization, Official Declaration 2, which ended the priesthood and temple restrictions, was also surrounded by a profound silence in the LDS Church's official channels. Church leaders "were instructed . . . to let the announcement speak for itself," and the First Presidency specifically did *not* make themselves available for media interviews following the announcement of the revelation.[77] That silence functioned, in part, as a way to strategically forget the church's problematic racial legacy—to consign it, if you will, to the dustbin of history.[78]

Jane's story fills the silence, redirecting attention to the historical presence of black members in the church. But in many ways, it seems like that silence seeped into narrations of Jane's life, making it nearly impossible to deal straightforwardly with the Church's history of racism and the ways that racism shaped Jane's experience. The Jane who emerges in these narratives is comfortable: even when she comes across as exotic and primitive, she is not threatening. She welcomes white Latter-day Saints rather than disquieting them. She allows church members to forget the church's historical racism and instead affirm their regard for, and even their spiritual connections to, the church's African American members, articulating an attitude of racial inclusivity and unity, rather than the racial division that the priesthood and temple restrictions had previously imposed.

At the same time, Jane's story also casts a spotlight on the church's ideals of femininity and family, projecting the principles of the "Proclamation on the Family" back into the church's history and highlighting them as a legacy to be carried forward. Cleansed of her sexual improprieties, rendered a loving, faithful wife of only one husband and a spiritual mother to all who need her, Jane appears as the matriarch of a devoted, stable family—the sort of family that the "Proclamation" envisions as ideal and declares as a norm for the twenty-first century church. As a model of LDS femininity, Jane allows the LDS Church to imagine the ideals of the Proclamation as having been a part of church teachings since the beginning. The family and gender roles that the Proclamation describes thus appear timeless, rather than as recognizable products of their own time.

What might these narratives look like if Jane's story was told in all its messy detail, rather than fit into neat twenty-first-century boxes? Narrators would have to grapple with race—not by invoking stereotypes, but by thinking about the ways an ideology of white supremacy shaped Jane's life and religious experiences.[79] And they would not find comfort in a racially egalitarian prophet. Instead, they would confront the fact that Joseph Smith himself was uncomfortable with racial difference at times. Instead of seeing in Jane a model of faithful femininity that transcends history, narrators might recognize the ways Jane did and did not live up to the feminine ideals of her time—and the ways her husband Isaac, denied the priesthood, was barred from embodying even the most basic masculine ideals of the church.[80] Far from taking refuge in the notion that Jane knew "families are forever"[81] and that "temple work . . . has [now] . . . been done for Jane and her family,"[82] they might wrestle with the ways religious institutions can cause profound pain: they might recognize that at the end of her life, with most of her children having left the church and predeceased her, Jane did not "go on her way rejoicing," as her monument implies. No, she begged for temple ceremonies. She had no priesthood holder in her family.[83] She desperately wanted to be sealed to her loved ones, not to be alone in eternity. Instead, she was sealed to Joseph Smith as a servant.

Jane's life, in this telling, is much less comfortable and certainly much less accessible. But a less sanitized rendering of her life is more human. It reveals how the experience of blackness, the norms of femininity, the construction of families, and the practice of Mormonism have changed, and how they have remained the same. And perhaps it might break that silence surrounding the institutional racism of the church, enabling a more complete reckoning with the LDS Church's racial past.

Acknowledgments

I am deeply grateful to numerous people for their help in the preparation of this essay. My writing group at the University of Wyoming—Erin Forbes, Teena Gabrielson, and Frieda Knobloch—have read and thoughtfully critiqued numerous versions of this essay. Ann Braude and several members of my Young Scholars in American Religion cohort read an early draft of this work and helped me think through some of my key ideas. Judith Weisenfield invited me to participate in a 2014 conference, "Race and Religion in American History," where I presented the first recognizable version of this essay and received valuable feedback from all of the conference participants. Brandi Hughes, Sarah Imhoff, and Rachel Lindsey read and critiqued a later iteration, and Sara M. Patterson and W. Paul Reeve read and vastly improved the draft version of this essay in lecture form. I am grateful to Philip Barlow and the rest of the Arrington Lecture committee for the invitation to speak, and to Brad Cole and the excellent staff in Special Collections and Archives at Merrill-Cazier Library, Utah State University, for arranging every last detail of the event with skill and grace. Finally, I thank Michael Spooner and the staff of Utah State University Press for making the publication process so pleasant.

Notes

1   Leonard J. Arrington, *Great Basin Kingdom: Economic History of the Latter-Day Saints, 1830–1900* (Lincoln: University of Nebraska Press, 1958).

2   There is an extensive literature on the position of blacks in early Utah. A good overview is W. Paul Reeve, *Religion of a Different Color: Race and the Mormon Struggle for Whiteness* (New York: Oxford University Press, 2015), 142–61.

3   Because Jane's surname changed multiple times, I will refer to her throughout this essay by her first name. For ease of reading, I have corrected spelling and punctuation of nineteenth-century quotations throughout this essay.

4   This summary of Jane's life is largely based on her autobiography, Jane Manning James, "Jane Manning James Autobiography" (Salt Lake City, Utah, n.d.), MS 4425, LDS Church History Library; and Henry J. Wolfinger, "A Test of Faith: Jane Elizabeth James and the Origins of the Utah Black Community," in *Social Accommodation in Utah*, ed. Clark S. Knowlton, American West Center Occasional Papers (Salt Lake City: University of Utah, 1975), 126–72. For a fully edited and annotated version of the major sources James left behind regarding her life story, see Quincy D. Newell, "The Autobiography and Interview of Jane Elizabeth Manning James," *Journal of Africana Religions* 1, no. 2 (2013): 251–91.

5   Newell, "The Autobiography and Interview of Jane Elizabeth Manning James," 269.

6   Ibid., 265.

7   Janet Ellingson, "Becoming a People: The Beliefs and Practices of the Early Mormons, 1830–1845" (Ph.D. dissertation, University of Utah, 1997). For discussion of the disincentivizing of ecstatic experience, see Stapley and Wright's discussion of women's healing in late nineteenth century Mormonism, Jonathan A. Stapley and Kristine Wright, "Female Ritual Healing in Mormonism," *Journal of Mormon History* 37, no. 1 (Winter 2011): 1–85.

8   Elizabeth J. D. Roundy reported this claim in a postscript to Jane's autobiography, which Roundy recorded. See Newell, "The Autobiography and Interview of Jane Elizabeth Manning James," 268.

9   Elias Smith, *Jane E. James v. Isaac James* (Salt Lake County Probate Court 1870) [Salt Lake County Probate Court records, Series 373, Reel 19, Box 14, Folder 046, Utah State Archives. March Term 1870, Hon. Elias Smith, Judge. Jane E. James vs. Isaac James, Bill for Divorce and Alimony.] I am grateful to Connell O'Donovan for pointing me to this source.

10   Emily Dow Partridge Young, "Diary and Reminiscences," 27 January 1875, p. 11, MS 22253, LDS Church History Library.

11   Although no marriage record has been found yet, Wolfinger uses other evidence to build a case for Jane's marriage to Perkins. See Wolfinger, "A Test of Faith," 133 and 161n22. His evidence is corroborated by other documentation, such as "Record of Baptisms for the Dead for the Seed of Cain" (microfilm, Salt Lake City, Utah, September 3, 1875), Film 255,498, LDS Family History Library, in which Jane appears performing baptisms for her dead alongside Frank Perkins. Jane's access to these rituals suggests that church officials accepted her relationship with Perkins as legitimate. In Relief Society records from 1874 through 1876, Jane is referred to as both "Sister Perkins" and "Sister James." From 1877 on, Jane only appears with the surname "James." Eighth Ward, Liberty Stake, Eighth Ward Relief Society Minutes and Records (1867-1969), LDS Church History Library.

12   Jane was baptized for Susan Brown, a friend, in 1875. "Record of Baptisms for the Dead for the Seed of Cain." In 1888, she performed several more baptisms for her female relatives. Church

of Jesus Christ of Latter-day Saints, Logan Temple, "Baptisms for the Dead, 1884–1943," n.d., 320, Microfilm 0,177,847, LDS Family History Library.

13 The largest published collection of Jane's extant petitions is in Wolfinger, "A Test of Faith," 148–51.

14 Gordon Irving, "The Law of Adoption: One Phase of the Development of the Mormon Concept of Salvation, 1830–1900," *Brigham Young University Studies* 14 (Spring 1974): 310.

15 On LDS discomfort with interracial relationships, see Reeve, *Religion of a Different Color*, 145–48, 158–59, 185–86.

16 The official record of the ritual is Adoption Record, Book A, p. 26, LDS Church History Library. This source is restricted and therefore not available to most researchers. I have examined photographs of this document. A reasonably accurate transcription is available in Devery S. Anderson, ed., *The Development of LDS Temple Worship, 1846-2000: A Documentary History*, Smith–Pettit Foundation Book (Salt Lake City: Signature Books, 2011), 97–98.

17 Minutes of a Meeting of the Council of the Twelve Apostles, January 2, 1902, transcribed in Wolfinger, "A Test of Faith," 151.

18 Kate B. Carter, *The Story of the Negro Pioneer* (Salt Lake City, Utah: Daughters of Utah Pioneers, 1965); Wolfinger, "A Test of Faith."

19 Examples include, but are certainly not limited to Ivan J. Barrett, *Heroic Mormon Women* (American Fork, Utah: Covenant Communications, 2000); Margaret Blair Young and Darius Aidan Gray, *One More River to Cross*, Standing on the Promises 1 (Salt Lake City: Bookcraft, 2000); Margaret Blair Young and Darius Aidan Gray, *Bound for Canaan*, Standing on the Promises 2 (Salt Lake City, Utah: Bookcraft, 2002); Margaret Blair Young and Darius Aidan Gray, *The Last Mile of the Way*, Standing on the Promises 3 (Salt Lake City, Utah: Bookcraft/ Deseret Book Co., 2003); "A Stranger in Nauvoo," *Provident Living*, March 2004; Scott Young Freebairn and Hey You Pictures, *Jane Manning James: Your Sister in the Gospel* (Layton, Utah: Hey You Pictures, 2005); Christy Karras, *More than Petticoats: Remarkable Utah Women* (Guilford, Conn.: Morris Book Publishing, 2010); and Elspeth Young, *Till We Meet Again*, oil paint, 2013.

20 Jane's story works differently—or perhaps it performs additional functions—for black Latter-day Saints, who are not my focus in this essay. On black LDS uses of Jane's story, see Max Perry Mueller, "Playing Jane: Re-Presenting Black Mormon Memory through Reenacting the Black Mormon Past," *Journal of Africana Religions* 1, no. 4 (2013): 513–61.

21 Curtis J. Evans, *The Burden of Black Religion* (Oxford; New York: Oxford University Press, 2008), 6–7, 107–10.

22 Linda King Newell and Valeen Tippetts Avery, "Jane Manning James: Black Saint, 1847 Pioneer," *Ensign*, August 1979, 26–29. Manuscript copies of this article are deposited in both Newell's papers, at the University of Utah, and Avery's papers, at Utah State University. I am grateful to Clint Pumphrey, Manuscript Curator, Special Collections and Archives, Utah State University; and Julia Huddleston, Archivist, J. Williard Marriott Library, Special Collections, University of Utah, for providing me with copies of the relevant documents from both collections.

23 *Ensign* began publication in 1971 as the official English-language church magazine for adults. In May 1986, its circulation was 477,000 copies. "News of the Church: Church Magazines Pass 1 Million Circulation," *Ensign*, June 1987, https://www.lds.org/ensign/1987/06/news-of-the -church/church-magazines-pass-1-million-circulation?lang=eng.

24 Examples include, but are not limited to, Joseph Walker, "Jane Elizabeth Manning James," in *Pioneer: Sesquicentennial, 1847–1997* (Midvale, Utah: Olympus Publishers, 1997), 26–29; Jane McBride Choate, "Jane Elizabeth Manning James," *Friend*, September 1997, https://www .lds.org/friend/1997/09?lang=eng; and Barrett, *Heroic Mormon Women*.

25 According to the article's endnotes, Newell and Avery consulted the following sources on James's life: James, "Jane Manning James Autobiography"; Wolfinger, "A Test of Faith"; Jane Elizabeth Manning James, "A Reminiscence of Joseph Smith," *Dialogue: A Journal of Mormon Thought* 5, no. 2 (Summer 1970): 128–30; and Carter, *The Story of the Negro Pioneer*.

26   In fact, the editors at *Ensign* suggested changes to the manuscript to ensure that the question of Sylvester's paternity did not occur to readers. The original manuscript referred to "Jane's eldest son, Sylvester." The editors responded, "Suggest deleting 'eldest' even though that was the case. Knowing Jane and Isaac James' first son was Silas and no earlier husband is given, it is a shock to see Sylvester mentioned as the eldest son." Linda King Newell Papers, Ms 447, Special Collections and Archives, J. Willard Marriott Library, University of Utah.

27   I have examined all available manuscript copies of this article, along with its published version. The omissions I enumerate here apply to all versions to which I have had access. Ibid.; Linda King Newell and Valeen Tippetts Avery, "Jane Elizabeth Manning James: Black Saint, Forgotten Pioneer," Valeen T. Avery Research Files, Coll. Mss 316, Box 12, Fd. 1, Special Collections and Archives, Utah State University.

28   The original subtitle of the article was "Black Saint, Forgotten Pioneer." By the time it was submitted to *Ensign*, it bore the subtitle with which it was published. Linda King Newell Papers.

29   Jane reported her early experience with glossolalia in her autobiography. See Newell, "The Autobiography and Interview of Jane Elizabeth Manning James," 263. Reports of Jane speaking in tongues at Retrenchment Society meetings appear in the following sources: Unsigned, "Semi-Monthly Meeting," *Woman's Exponent*, December 1, 1889; Lydia D. Alder, "Ladies' Semi-Monthly Meeting," *Woman's Exponent*, December 1, 1893; Lydia D. Alder, "Ladies' Semi-Monthly Meeting," *Woman's Exponent*, June 1, 1894; Lydia D. Alder, "Ladies' Semi-Monthly Meeting," *Woman's Exponent*, January 1, 1895; Lydia D. Alder, "Ladies' Semi-Monthly Meeting," *Woman's Exponent*, June 1, 1897; J. S. Woolley, "Ladies' Semi-Monthly Meeting," *Woman's Exponent*, July 1, 1899; J. S. Woolley, "Ladies' Semi-Monthly Meeting," *Woman's Exponent*, October 15, 1899.

30   Newell, "The Autobiography and Interview of Jane Elizabeth Manning James," 264; Lydia D. Alder, "Ladies' Semi-Momthly [*sic*] Meeting," *Woman's Exponent*, December 15, 1896.

31   Newell, "The Autobiography and Interview of Jane Elizabeth Manning James," 265.

32   Ellingson, "Becoming a People"; Lee Copeland, "Speaking in Tongues in the Restoration Churches," *Dialogue: A Journal of Mormon Thought* 24, no. 1 (Spring 1991): 13–33.

33   Copeland, "Speaking in Tongues," 27.

34   Ibid., 21 quoting Pratt, 1884.

35   Newell, "The Autobiography and Interview of Jane Elizabeth Manning James," 264.

36   On the decline of ecstatic practices in Mormonism, see Stapley and Wright, "Female Ritual Healing," and Copeland, "Speaking in Tongues," among others.

37   Newell and Avery, "Jane Manning James," 26.

38   Ibid., 28, 29.

39   Ibid., 29.

40   Ibid.

41   Newell and Avery did make the claim in the article that Walker Lewis was one of Jane's suitors in Nauvoo, though the only evidence for this assertion is Jane's later request to be sealed to Lewis. Ibid., 28. Interestingly, in early drafts of the article, Newell and Avery referred to Lewis as a "black elder." By the time the article was published, the phrasing had been changed to "black man." See Newell and Avery, "Jane Elizabeth Manning James: Black Saint, Forgotten Pioneer"; Newell, "Linda King Newell Papers."

42   Newell and Avery, "Jane Manning James," 29.

43   Ibid., 26.

44   Ibid., 28, quoting Joseph Smith, *History of the Church*, 6:205.

45   Ibid.

46   Ibid., 29.

47   In his introduction to a brief text on African American religion, Eddie S. Glaude argues that "African American religion emerges in the encounter between faith, in all of its complexity, and white supremacy." See Glaude, *African American Religion: A Very Short Introduction*, Very Short Introductions 397 (New York: Oxford University Press, 2014), 6.

48   On Johnson, see Mary L. Bradford, "All on Fire: An Interview with Sonia Johnson," *Dialogue: A Journal of Mormon Thought* 14, no. 2 (Summer 1981): 27–47.

49   Newell and Avery, "Jane Manning James," 29, quoting James's biography; compare with Newell, "The Autobiography and Interview of Jane Elizabeth Manning James," 267–68.

50   This instance of Jane's generosity is documented in Eliza Lyman's journal. Lyman's words were quoted in Kate Carter's biographical sketch of Jane. See Scott H. Partridge, ed., *Eliza Maria Partridge Journal* (Provo, Utah: Grandin Book Company, 2003), 49; and Carter, *The Story of the Negro Pioneer*, 9.

51   Jane Elizabeth Manning James monument, Salt Lake City Cemetery, Utah. I use sentence case (rather than all capital letters) here, but otherwise I have chosen to reproduce the text and punctuation of the monument precisely in this quotation without including [sic] markings. I trust the reader will recognize the statement that Jane was born in 1882, and the inconsistencies in punctuation, as typographical errors.

52   Alexander B. Morrison, "Dedication Remarks and Dedicatory Prayer," April 1, 2005. The Genesis Group webpage where I originally found Morrison's remarks is no longer available, but an archived copy of it may be found at https://web.archive.org/web/20130402233912/http ://www.ldsgenesisgroup.org/archivenews/morrison.html.

53   LDS Church First Presidency, "The Family: A Proclamation to the World," https://www.lds .org/topics/family-proclamation?lang=eng.

54   Ibid.

55   E.E. Evans-Pritchard offers a thorough overview of Western takes on "primitive religion" in the introduction to his *Theories of Primitive Religion* (New York: Oxford University Press, 1965), 1–19.

56   Diane Roberts, *The Myth of Aunt Jemima: Representations of Race and Region* (New York: Routledge, 1994), 10; Evans, *The Burden of Black Religion*, 7.

57   Pioneer Chapter of the National Society of the Sons of Utah Pioneers, "Days of '47 Sunrise Service Program," July 25, 2005, copy in my possession.

58   This line comes directly from Young and Gray, *One More River to Cross*, 97. Although I do not discuss the bulk of Young and Gray's work in this essay, they have been very influential in shaping Jane's image in LDS discourse.

59   On the Mammy figure, see Micki McElya, *Clinging to Mammy: The Faithful Slave in Twentieth-Century America* (Cambridge, Mass.: Harvard University Press, 2007); and Roberts, *The Myth of Aunt Jemima*, among others.

60   Pioneer Chapter of the National Society of the Sons of Utah Pioneers, "Days of '47 Sunrise Service Program."

61   Curtis J. Evans notes that at some points in American history, white Northerners "found blacks a convenient symbol to point out what their society lacked, and romantic images of African Americans became a means of mediating the spiritual experience of whites." See Evans, *The Burden of Black Religion*, 6–7.

62   Patrick Sherry attributes the general idea of disenchantment to sociologist Max Weber, who used this concept in several of his major works. Patrick Sherry, "Disenchantment, Re-Enchantment, and Enchantment," *Modern Theology* 25, no. 3 (July 2009): 369–72.

63   Church of Jesus Christ of Latter-day Saints, "New Pageant to Premiere in Historic Nauvoo," www.mormonnewsroom.org, June 10, 2005, http://www.mormonnewsroom.org/article/new -pageant-to-premiere-in-historic-nauvoo.

64   T.C. Christensen and Gary Cook, *Joseph Smith: The Prophet of the Restoration* (LDS Motion Picture Studio, 2005), https://www.lds.org/media-library/ video/2011-03-01-joseph-smith-the-prophet-of-the-restoration?lang=eng.

65   Stanley Harrold, *Border War: Fighting over Slavery before the Civil War* (Chapel Hill: University of North Carolina Press, 2010), 3–7.

66   Richard L. Bushman, *Joseph Smith: Rough Stone Rolling* (New York: Alfred A. Knopf, 2005), 4–5, 516–17.

67   Christensen and Cook, *Joseph Smith: The Prophet of the Restoration.*
68   Quincy D. Newell, "'Is There No Blessing for Me?' Jane James's Construction of Space in Latter-Day Saint History and Practice," in *New Perspectives in Mormon Studies: Creating and Crossing Boundaries*, ed. Quincy D. Newell and Eric F. Mason (Norman: University of Oklahoma Press, 2013), especially 51–58.
69   Pioneer Chapter of the National Society of the Sons of Utah Pioneers, "Days of '47 Sunrise Service Program."
70   Susan Easton Black, "Honoring Jane Manning James: Courage on a Stage of Bigotry," *Segullah*, Fall 2005, http://www.segullah.org/fall2005/honoringjane.html.
71   James H. Cone, *Black Theology and Black Power*, An Original Seabury Paperback, SP 59 (New York: Seabury Press, 1969), 68.
72   Toni Morrison, "Comment," *The New Yorker*, October 5, 1998, http://www.newyorker.com/magazine/1998/10/05/comment-6543.
73   Cone, *Black Theology and Black Power*, 69.
74   Morrison, "Comment."
75   Kathleen Flake, "Re-Placing Memory: Latter-Day Saint Use of Historical Monuments and Narrative in the Early Twentieth Century," *Religion and American Culture: A Journal of Interpretation* 13, no. 1 (Winter 2003): 71.
76   Ibid., 71–72.
77   Edward L. Kimball, "Spencer W. Kimball and the Revelation on Priesthood," *BYU Studies* 47, no. 2 (2008): 66.
78   On the continuing silence surrounding Official Declaration 2, and the First Presidency's refusal to repudiate the racial folklore of the church or apologize for previous racism, see Armand L. Mauss, *All Abraham's Children: Changing Mormon Conceptions of Race and Lineage* (Urbana, Ill: University of Illinois Press, 2003), 248–250.
79   Glaude, *African American Religion*, 6–10.
80   Amy Hoyt and Sara M. Patterson, "Mormon Masculinity: Changing Gender Expectations in the Era of Transition from Polygamy to Monogamy, 1890–1920," *Gender & History* 23, no. 1 (April 1, 2011): 73.
81   The phrase "families are forever" has long been popular in the LDS Church. A quick search for the phrase on the LDS Church website yields dozens of hits stretching back to at least 1973. See "The Family Home Evening Manual: Starting Point for 'Forever Families,'" *Ensign*, https://www.lds.org/ensign/1973/09/the-family-home-evening-manual-starting-point-for-forever-families?lang=eng.
82   Newell and Avery, "Jane Manning James," 29.
83   On the ways the priesthood restriction affected black families, see especially O. Kendall White, Jr., "Boundary Maintenance, Blacks, and the Mormon Priesthood," *The Journal of Religious Thought* 37 (Fall-Winter 1980–81): 44.